T0303567

Charles Olson
The Principle of Measure
in Composition by Field:
Projective Verse II

Charles Olson

The Principle of Measure

in Composition by Field:

Projective Verse II

Edited by Joshua Hoeynck

chax press

Tucson 2010

Manuscript of "Projective Verse II," from the Charles Olson Research Collection. Archives and Special Collections at the Thoomas J. Dodd Research Center, University of Connecticut Libraries.

Manuscript of "Notes on Poetics," from the Charles Olson Research Collection. Archives and Special Collections at the Thomas J. Dodd Research Center, University of Connecticut Libraries.

ISBN 978 0925904 95 9

Published by
Chax Press
411 N 7th Ave Ste 103
Tucson, AZ 85705-8388
USA

Printed in Canada by Friesens

INTRODUCTION

Perusing Olson's manuscripts entitled "The Principle of Measure in Composition by Field: Projective Verse II" and "Notes on Poetics (toward Projective Verse II)," readers may recall one of Olson's claims in "Projective Verse." At the outset, he points American poets away from "the NON-Projective," "'closed verse,' that verse which print bred and which is pretty much what we have had, in English & American, and have still got, despite the work of Pound & Williams" (CP, 239). Implying a tense attitude toward his poetic influences, Olson's comment may suggest Pound and Williams write projective verse. Alternatively, he may intimate their achievements fail to shake poetics loose of the strict metric forms "bred" when "print" caused Modern English to replace the vernacular. "Projective Verse II" clarifies the matter, containing no references to Pound while lauding Williams' short story, "The Burden of Loveliness." Though studies often use Olson's statement from "Projective Verse" to link him to Pound and Williams, the appearance of "Projective Verse II" will add a third name to the list of Olson's influences: the English mathematician and philosopher, Alfred North Whitehead.

Whitehead (1861-1947) maintains a commanding presence in twentieth century philosophy. After gaining recognition for his mathematical work with Bertrand Russell, *Principia Mathematica* (1910-1913), he moved to Harvard University in 1924, teaching and developing his process philosophy. He then delivered his magnum opus, *Process and Reality*, as the 1927 Gifford Lectures at Edinburgh University. In *Process and Reality*, Whitehead contemplates the philosophies of Descartes, Locke, Hume, and Kant, disputing their metaphysical schemes and imagining a cosmos of co-dependent things, a universe dominated by relations. The later chapters outline how processes of abstraction like scientific measurement can objectify the world's variety of interrelated occasions. Throughout "Notes on Poetics

(Toward Projective Verse II)," Olson works mainly from Whitehead's chapter entitled "Strains," attempting to form Whitehead's terminology into a theory of quantitative metrics. In the actual essay, "The Principle of Measure in Composition by Field: Projective Verse II," he works from Whitehead's chapter entitled "Measurement." The two chapters close the fourth part of *Process and Reality*, "The Theory of Extension," in which Whitehead details his geometric and scientific positions regarding connections, measurement, and perception. By drafting his essays from these two chapters, Olson transforms the vocabulary of Whitehead's philosophy of science into a language for metrics and quantitative verse, thereby casting the projective mode as an observational poetics engaging with things, environments, and the heterogeneity of the actual world, what Olson names "the variety of order in creation" in the opening proposition of "Projective Verse II."

Though it true to say that these essays probably will not attain the same stature as "Projective Verse" in critical considerations of Olson's career, they should prove useful for explicating several poems in *Maximus*. In the "Notes," for instance, Olson defines his sense of Whitehead's terms "strain" and "strain-locus," both of which appear in poems like "Maximus From Dogtown IV" and "The island, the river, the shore" (II. 163; III. 209). Deploying Whitehead's terms from the chapter titled "Measurement" in "the Mountain of no difference," a late poem in *Maximus III*, Olson takes up Whitehead's critique of systematic modes of measurement by citing Whitehead's use of pure mathematics in the "Theory of Extension":

> "throughout the system"
> modulus precise finite segments
> -"There are no infinitesimals"
> all does rhyme like is the measure of
> producing like (III.124)

Disregarding the implicit reference to Jung's notion of like producing like, we can now tell the entire story about how these lines transform Whitehead's claim that the mathematical integral which stands for the property of distance depends on the faulty concept of an infinitesimal, a limit such as a point. In *Process and Reality*, Whitehead argues that modern procedures of measurement neglect the fact "that there are no infinitesimals, and that a comparison of finite segments is thus required" (*PR*, 332). Next, he suggests that in order to compare these finite segments without infinitesimals, thereby to seize the nature of the world's relations, mathematicians and scientists require a new integral, which he names "impetus, suggestive of [the integral's] physical import" (*PR*, 332-333). Though the term "impetus" is central to Whitehead's quarrel with Einstein's theory of relativity, the scientific community largely ignores Whitehead's objections. Nonetheless, Olson productively and poetically deploys the term in "Projective Verse II." He defines the "first magnitude of projective verse" as "length," employing Whitehead's concept of "precise finite segments," and the "second magnitude" as "impetus," eliciting attention to how the physical "manifold" or what he calls "whatever comes to hand" influences rhythm and form. Hence, "the Mountain of no difference" builds on Whitehead's critique of systematic modes of measurement by asserting the primacy of "rhyme," that is, physical multiplicity creates harmonious yet inexplicable experiences – "all does rhyme" – even though microscopic measurements cannot affix an exact number to a line. For Olson, Whitehead's identification of the incongruence between measured object and measuring tool applies to quantitative verse; thus one cannot attach a precise duration for each spoken vowel sound.

Despite the expanded perspective that these essays will offer for Olson's poems, the larger significance of "Projective Verse II" is up for debate. How does one take the measure of an unpublished essay that, on one extreme, radically changes or, on the other, merely adds to the received understanding of Olson's poetics from "Projective Verse" (1950)? Olson's "Kingfishers" offers the most compelling answer: "What does not change / is the will to change." Exploring the archive, the Olson scholar discovers various materials that influence Olson's poetry, which embraces change, uncertainty, doubt, the state of negative capability that comes when a writer gives himself or herself over to the materials of experience and knowledge. It is unsurprising, then, that Olson, a poet who sensitively registers the relations between the evolving

11

properties of the cosmos and the mind, should change projective verse upon discovering Whitehead's suggestion that "There is nothing in the real world which is merely an inert fact. Every reality is there for feeling: it promotes feeling; and it is felt" (*PR*, 310). Indeed, readers immersed in Olson's poems know well the metaphysical principles behind *Maximus*: the grand and inexplicable system of relations governing the cosmos – "sewn in & binding / each seam" – dictates materials collide and synthesize with other materials to create new relations that cause one to feel this ordered yet indescribable pluriverse (*M*, 564). These interests – relation, change, process – made Olson's mind gravitate to Whitehead's process philosophy, which systematizes the proposition that "we find ourselves in a buzzing world, amid a democracy of fellow creatures" (*PR*, 50).

While the two essays published here show the extent of Olson and Whitehead's shared intellectual adventure into observing that "buzzing world" and attempting to objectify it, the fact remains that Olson withheld the essays from publication. On January 22nd of 1958, he wrote to Robert Creeley and described "The Principle of Measure in Composition by Field: Projective Verse II" as an "opus (on Verse)," indicating its importance for his poetry. So, why not publish? Olson's correspondence from the late fifties with Don Allen provides the precise answer. On January 11th of 1958, he wrote to Allen that "The Pro Verse piece (II) is done" and discussed Allen's plans to publish it in the *Evergreen Review* (*Poet to Publisher*, 23). Two and a half months later, he again wrote to Allen: "I shall continue to labor on the 2nd pro verse thing, but looking it over that night I continue to feel it needs clearing from the Old Wise Head" (*Poet to Publisher*, 30). Here, Olson jokingly puns on Whitehead's name, revealing his concern that his inheritance from process philosophy made his ideas too derivative. Nevertheless, the essay's unpublished status does not make it irrelevant precisely because it displays Olson's consistent attempt to refine his ideas, expand his repertoire of usable materials, and celebrate how the actual world induces a poem's agency, which then directs the writer. When he states that projective verse "has one law: it has to occur. And to occur it has to retain and create its own environment," readers should discover cause for Olson's many poems written en plein air in *Maximus III*. Similarly, when he names "a principle of measure" in composition by field "least action," a term from Whitehead which Olson takes to mean "least subjective action," readers might hear Olson's rejection of the expression of personal, subjective actions in poems. Developed in *Maximus III*, the notion of a poetics of "least action" accounts for lines such as "I am a ward / and precinct / man myself and hate / universalization, believe / it only feeds into a class of deteriorated / personal lives anyway," that is, "The Big False Humanism / Now on" (III.11).

The actual essay, "The Principle of Measure in Composition by Field: Projective Verse II," is seven typed manuscript pages, ending with a footnote that bows to Whitehead's *Process and Reality*. "Notes on Poetics (Toward Projective Verse II)" is hand-written in a notebook contained in a folder at Storrs titled "A poem is a presented duration as such it involves rest, speed & acceleration." Since one of Olson's editors typed both essays, I have transcribed the material using the editorial typescripts and Olson's original manuscripts. My thirty-three endnotes point interested readers toward the pertinent source material within *Process and Reality*, using Olson's underlinings and annotations while also detailing the steps of his writing process. I would like to thank the staff at the University of Connecticut, Storrs, particularly Melissa Watterworth for allowing the publication of these essays. To Steven Meyer, my dissertation adviser, I owe an enormous debt. I also thank Chax Press and Charles Alexander for publishing these essays. Lastly, on this occasion, the Centennial celebration of Olson's birth, I should note it is good for us, a polis of poets and scholars, to come together acknowledging a life lived so passionately for poetics. Olson's archive contains enough unpublished material that will keep us editing, researching, and chasing after his ideas for many years.

THE PRINCIPLE OF MEASURE
IN
COMPOSITION BY FIELD

(PROJECTIVE VERSE – Part II)

1 The poem's job is to be able to attend, and to get attention to, the variety of order in creation

1.1 It does this for two reasons: that the requisites for experience be increased, both for whoever reads, and for creation itself, which awaits each novel advance men make as further evidence of herself.[1]

1.2 The other reason is that all creation is also obstructive. This has been called evil of her. However, there is another craving: to put an end to obstruction by bringing into existence a thing which shall be lucid, and also of immediate worth. Such as a work of art.[2]

2 That any of the above get done requires the poet to be as skillful as his desire. Wherefore a principle of measure can be offered

2.1 It is 'least action' – viz., least song[3]

2.2 It is 'least in order to insure that the condition variety shall rapidly recur on the lucid as it does on the obstructive plane – in other words that the condition adhered to in the prior shall be the truth of the consequent as well

2.3 Variety, whether systematic or random, fast or slow, happens to present itself in a domain (which was defined for the first time in the year Moby Dick was written). In that year Riemann characterized the continuous as 'the domain of the infinitely small.' (A moment's reflection will satisfy that all that does happen to us happens via the infinitely small.)[4]

3 Technically, 'least' works out this way. A poem is a 'line' between any two points in creation (the poem's beginning, and its end). In its passage it includes – in the

3.1 meaning here it passes through – the material of itself. Such a material is the 'field,' and in verse has the function of an integral which shall be called 'impetus.' The problem of the poem, therefore, is that the impetus of the material (the differential element of) and the systematic length (the poem from beginning to end) shall constitute a successful composition.

3.2 This is only possible if both line and field stay weighted with the individual peculiarities of the poem's relevant environment – its idiosyncratic quality of being itself, of being 'obstructive' at the same time that it is lucid, and of immediate worth. This is the double which reality itself only has eternally. And statement does not have. It is the poem's peculiar province in non-Euclidean discourse.[5]

We have, therefore, three magnitudes of a poem, in all of which the principle of 'least action' does apply and is to be understood:

the 'line' of the poem (which would previously have been called its 'form' – what it is, from beginning to end);

its material or 'field', here called 'impetus'; and

its condition as intrinsic to itself, that by which this poem differs from all other poems which have been or might be written, what can be called its own 'obstructiveness'

II

(Notes, on last above:

"<u>length</u>"

A poem is 'heard' before it is written, and until it ends. So its prosody is a dictum: there is no form until the poem creates its own

The poem, from the moment it starts, is a line: it goes between two points. There is no alternative. It behaves itself. There is a judge. The inspection of the poet is half the case, the other half is what's true, willy-nilly of the poet.[6] How things are. There is no wallabying. Or yabbering. It is 'taste.' In the vocabulary here used, the differential, <u>systematic</u> length: how far to go, what proportion represents <u>the</u> proportion of the material in hand. In the non-Euclidean world there is no prior discourse – no statement, or rule – by which the poem rests.[7] There is no 'universal' either of prepared form (mold) or of "thought" on which it may lean. Or get run. It leans solely (it doesn't lean) on the sharpest outline (gravure, bounds) it can manage for itself.

It can draw from the variety of order in the world. It sure does. It can't help but. It has no choice. But no randomness, or any least traffic with the chaotic. No matter how much the 'line' may seem to wander, in getting home.

It is the most clear business, the line, of a poem

"<u>impetus</u>"

Most of where the 'writing' is (?) Or rewriting, getting it to go. The disadvantage (loss from the closed poem) is no rule of how what does go in should be tucked (the

17

manifold, in). Very much "behaving," to unknown 'laws' of whatever comes to hand. It might drag. It may or may not 'talk.' It might sleep. It also might sing. Or appear to go all off what you might expect a poem to do – in this respect appear to contradict its very imperative of a poem with line, show harmony, reflect rhythm.

Go blind. Why quantity is the only measure (any qualitative even the obvious pleasure or even the self-creating powers of language itself, when one can write, sometime to be sacrificed. Very hard.)

Cf. quantity, below

Most 'composition,' in field: as, say, Webern, to tree trunk, catching it as catch can, or how was it the poet had it it mouses through the grass no blade, stirs; whatever's your cup, Zen, the nation, the next rumble – or tea

"crass"

Content. Pure & simple. Dirty. The peculiarities, of the poem's environment. Literally. "Make it dirty" (WCW, to his wife, at the door, announcing a new 5th book to Patterson). That they be stuck to. "It's gonna be dirty, Flossie" (how he gets the "Burden of Loveliness," a best example yet of quantity (as story the which the Russians, the great Russians, do not equal)

It's the easiest to write about, this magnitude, content. If not to do. Thanks, say, to Dante. Plus what's happened since 1821 or whatever year it was John Keats said, "Negative Capability," about which year Lobatschewsky and Bolyai Janos 1000 miles apart kicked the struts out from under the old universe of discourse in knocking out the geometry of the Greek-to-then system.

One can talk of a vernacular world, once space

is not a sphere but a wrap-around, a funny face from the
five and ten, an elastic bound idly around a pencil – when
alternatives, in quantics, are provable. "I mean staying,"
said John Keats, "in a condition of symbolization, mystery,
and doubt, without any irritable reaching after fact and
reason," or about how he put it, challenging Coleridge.

What the poem thereafter has to do, is to keep
the conditions of obstruction out of which it comes, or it
will fall back into the split between universal and particular,
neither of which is any such thing. It cannot clear by
throwing overboard the whistles and baggages of its own
birthplace. It has one law: it has to occur. And to occur it
has to retain and create its own environment. Otherwise,
it lifts away, into culture. The muse of the vernacular
poem is history (as the Greek poem was under the sign of
astronomy – the labors of Zodiac, 12 stations 12 books;
agricultural art.) The poem was either agriculture or culture
before John Keats. It was why he had so much trouble.
Since him it has been science, what Dante only, previously,
seems to have been able to say:

"Comedy, is that kind of poetic narration differing from all
others because the end of the whole and the part may be
manifold, to wit, the proximate and the ultimate.

"It requires the vernacular, because the end is to remove
those living from the state of misery and lead them to a
prosperous end."

I am hearty here. One musn't mind. So much of writing
still is ladeedah – even when it's an inventory of a hipster's
cupboard of unholy actions well done and happy possession
of illegal things. It's so dull, the social – and democratic.
The pursuit of happiness. One craves one intuitive. Or one
contemplative.

Obstruction is the business of sticking the poem's nose into (the poet's) keeping its neck bent, into the places of its own coming-from. And it doesn't mean seriatim, realism, any catalogue or biography. It means the environment, that it be created. Where it came from as it goes whooping into its own non-applied existence and putativeness.

There is no content to which a poem is alien. None. Can that be heard?

Vernacular is what does not possess grammar until it does. Whatever turns up in one's hands as what one is writing from (one's nurse's milk, Dante called it. Leave it. Keep it there.

III

Quote:

> "The interweaving of the individual peculiarities of actual occasions [content] upon the background of systematic geometry [impetus]"

and

> "This systematic geometry expresses the 'substantial form' inherited throughout creation [which the poem as 'line' enters when the poem begins] which constitutes the primary real potentiality conditioning concrescence which is what the poem does when it brings its line successfully to its termination[8]

If these two quotations are grasped, the field poem throughout itself is understood.

I apply the terms:

"Actual Occasions": all that 'happens' – events, but persons, creatures, things, anywhere anytime, as well[9]

This would be the vernacular, from which and by which the poem keeps its density as well as out of which it draws its own clarity

Such 'occasions' are – and in the poet's hand are supposed to stay – individual and peculiar

'Systematic geometry': composition proper, the management of materials so that they tilt, hang, land, rise, go off, fall, weigh, ride, anything that anything does do – and bring it off.

The nature of the construction of the real

'substantial form': what the poem when it comes off is

IV

Why metric has had to change to do with quantity, the restoration of attention to the implicated character of the physical in everything. Quantity is the energy of matter (impetus. That all things flow can now be rewritten, and Heraclitus restored, an end put to Socratic error. All things are vectors, among them systematic order thrives. This is private truth as well. Feelings are vector, the vector character of them is fundamental.[10]

Like the man sd,

> "there isn't anything in the world which is inert fact,
> everything is there for feeling: it promotes feeling; and it
> is felt. And there is nothing which belongs merely to the
> privacy of one individual's feeling. All origination is private.
> But what has been thus originated publicly pervades the
> world."[11]

21

Quantity is both extensive and intensive.[12] In terms of the poem, for example, because all is vector no single thing (to syllable vowel or the letter of the syllable) doesn't tip on a balance reaching to the farthest out – outside the poem, way out; the poet's sensibility as well, if he is poised to be inclusive.[13] Which immediately shores (the extensive of quantity does) the decisiveness of the poem's bounds. What it includes is a decisive factor of what it excludes – how it hangs delicately in the midst of all physicality, surveying all objects. The poem's boundedness (it declares the inside of a poem, its volume) can be complete, because of quantity, in a sense denied to all outsideness. A vague sense of externality in a poem will not do, it betrays a not high organism in the poet.[14] The component variations in the poem have, in such a case, failed to differentiate themselves into grades of intensity.[15]

Intensity is as well quantitative as it is qualitative – as we have had the poet's nerves in poems, his sensitivity without necessarily any other thrust, any imbalance than, his sensitivity (which need do more than arouse our admiration, it being a sort of triumph the race might prize, that one be able to distinguish successfully among sensations.

Footnote to the end of PROJECTIVE VERSE II

It should be evident to anyone who knows his thought,
that in the foregoing I am completely appropriating
words and means of stating them from Alfred North
Whitehead. It has this advantage: to introduce into an
area in which only Dante has written with steady appeal
to common sense, a system of thought which throughout
itself makes the same appeal. It ought, therefore, to work
out that anyone who wishes to, can test what is here said
about verse by reference both to their own experience
and to a text where experience is carefully and completely
analyzed. I refer to Whitehead's <u>Process</u> <u>and</u> <u>Reality</u>.

I was late in finding out how good Whitehead is. I had
been asked by Hester Pickman to dinner to meet him
when I was younger. He was surrounded by those who
flutter about a man when he is older. I missed him. But
it didn't matter, for when I did get him, it was good
enough.

The non-Euclidean revolution receives in Whitehead
what undoes forever the unfortunate "universe of
discourse" which saddled man from Socrates to
Lubachevsky. He takes the universal and wrings its neck,
better than when Diogenes did, when he threw the hare
in the window of Plato's schoolroom saying, "Here,
children, is his idea of what a man is all about."[16]

Notes on Poetics
(toward Projective Verse II)

What I am proposing is a refreshment of our vocabulary
to deal with such matters as rhythm, meter, feet, forms (like
ode, etc.) all prosody. I would say, for example, that we junk
the notion of a meter proper to an accented language and that
the quantitative somehow is responsible outside an inflectional
tongue. So thoroughly has English moved over and of such
radicalness is the change above that we are better off starting
as though it was all as new as Greek to Homer, and English to
Chaucer.

Time in a poem, that is. It can be broken down into rest,
velocity, acceleration. Rest is a matter of duration. Velocity is rate
(of speed). Etc. But is time then only the verbalnesses? Or put it
the most forwarding way: on only word play is time playing in the
poem? What about the "substance" of the poem – the "thought,"
etc. Where's time here? Merely the philosophy of science (as
it so often well is only Ozymandias, & the extensions of that
wish, right through Mr. Eliot and on now into the young, out of
Thomas via Caitlin.[17]

Rest is place, occurs in space, as well as duration. Speed is
a speed of what – and why rev it, or decelerate – what occasion
excuses these time changes in the poem, this change-up?

Or the poet, where is he, in the poem? Because of the vector
character of everything how is he vector? For if, in the new
discourse, the poem (the object) cannot afford to be statement,
the poet – the "subject" – is equally not static (statable). As the
poem goes from a beginning just inside multiplicity to an end
in objectification, the subject (the poet) remains prior, excluding

and surviving, passing on after the poem to do another.[18] The duration of himself as an occasion is an infinite number, but the 'rest' of himself (his "time") in any given poem is the poem itself, not he. Or he will encumber the poem with himself, a time too dull for the occasion because unequal to it, improper to it, and not capable of the objectification it cries for – to die into, as love. The poet thus inside will leak out of the one thing which can cause the poem to be – the matter by which the strains of entity (quantitative time, the time of 'things,' murmurous wood, the stone wall as bench, peacocks carrying on down an alley, with grumpkins looking on, through the slits he will love that which can become present if multiplicity may be free – free from him.

***

There can be no duration (time of the poem) without materium – without the place where the strains are by which the enduring objects are made known.[19] They can be only known via a strain-locus, and I am here to offer it as 'home' for the poet as well as the poem.[20] Once a poet knows he can be in & out of the poem in proper part. Prior to it he acquired the poem. In it as person his only value is what he excludes. He survives the poem if he has been its servant – if as such (and never as himself) he has got the flawless necessary matter to it, and its words. Then he has shown, can hold it up to other men, substantial form; and he can go on to find again another proper occasion.

The poem's prosody (that which is accomplished by bringing about its end) has an aspect to it which, in the old discourse, there is no way or reason to recognize & thus grapple with. Fliply, it is what it ain't. But it can be stated for its import, which is considerable: it is that the poem carries in itself the evidence of what it isn't, as well as what it is. Thus acquiring to itself much more the power of power outside as well as, by this intensification

26

of its own knowledge itself, its own power.[21] That is, as in painting, the frame. All loss today, to conceive of the canvas in such self-isolation. But I am not here talking of the poem in its aspect of 'line' – of what it is inside the multiplicity it came out of, and the fact that it cannot be if it isn't cut off, in the end, as an object, itself. I am talking about the painting of the painting, how do you paint it, when the frame is not the limiting factor it once was. How do you write the poem when you do not want the poem to stay in – even though it has to, to be itself. How do you do this?

Other than do it: I am perfectly aware that is an answer, but it is also interesting to anyone who cares to know what it is that they are doing, and not only for the reason that they may do it more. In itself it brings one up against how Dante had it – the manifold.

I offer as the best image I know of at the moment, for the problem of composition in field, what Whitehead calls strain-locus. What he means by that can I believe be clearly and valuably applied to verse, and this same critical ground he established for practice and judgment. I quote: "There is nothing in the real world which is merely inert fact. Every reality is there for feeling: it promotes feeling; and it is felt. Also, there is nothing which belongs merely to the privacy of feeling of one individual actuality. All origination is private. But what has been thus originated, publicly pervades the world."

It is these public facts (and a poem is fairly such, yes?) which have therefore (because they do characterize the feelings) a 'geometry,' a structure of systematic order. A feeling, therefore, in which the forms concern such order, is (to take Whitehead's word, a 'strain.'

"In a strain," he goes on, "qualitative elements other than the geometrical forms, express themselves as qualities implicated in those forms" – which puts the quality question where it needs to be put, that it is not in its own statement or more delicate evidence (presence as beauty etc) that it has its place so much as that it expresses itself 'implicated' in the presiding forms of occurrence itself.[22]

A strain is characterized by the close association of qualities and definite geometrical relations, and a growth of ordered physical complexity (which ought to be the poem) is dependent on the growth of ordered relationships among strains.[23]

By strain I mean what happens literally to the body's geometry. You know, off-balance etc. The wit(ness) of the body, as well as any 'excitement.' Excitement is for the qualitative but the cool is sheer disturbance, unacknowledged by any heightening necessarily, any sign except that which the person knows inside is most. It is this order of change – of impetus – I am saying a quantitative poem reaches for, to produce. And has its art.

A strain-locus is merely an exceptional occasion of such effect – a poem, for example, by which a real change (and mind you, not qualitative) I mean a geometrical (that's for the physiologically) disturbance (shock – bust up the place – take over) takes over.

The character of this art is ultimate. For it happens to coincide with the way things are. I don't propose here to make the case. I wish only to pull anyone's attention to the fact, that if a poem is taken in its aspect as thing, and the qualitative is left where it always is, & has to be – implicated in the thing and only expressing itself by it – the power comes into the poet's hands.

But he has to place himself in the poem's hands, as thing, to do it. He cannot be fancy-pants. If he is agent, prior to the poem he acquires it. In the poem he is obedient. He survives the poem if he has been. He has got the flawless necessary matter of it. He has shown up its substantial form. He can go on to find another occasion.

The answers to those questions are in the men who achieve it. My purpose here is, once and for all, to get it named, to call what there is no reason not to preserve of what was classically quantitative, and can now, that language is far enough from those old debates, be stated for what it is: the amount of the poem. Why the song can be the least, that the matter is measured motion as well, the words are all they are, as well as their 'song.'

It is exciting to contemplate, because of what it entails – says in its own saying. For example, the physical. One is able today to mark where sensations are qualitative and that feelings are not so, they are the 4/5ths which lie under, they are – what 'physical' won't say – geometric. By that I mean structured as things are to the heart of themselves, and connected with each other, not simply impinging by rubbing on distance of surface from one another (where so much of imagery stays, as love or affrightment of superficies, reaching arms, etc., branches) when we are drawn driven torn thrown by forces of grab and refusal as strong & blind as what shakes the heart of the sun. One can call these things by name, strictly place them, offer them as sources of substance & act in poems.

I will be forgiven if I here stress the systematic and the geometrical just to get us on. It is not easy to invent these terms oneself. One knows the experience, one can do what the experience tells one to do, but to go outside the poet's own work – to try to wear the monkey-suit of thought – it is not so easy, or necessarily so wise. I am impelled I am surprised so little seems noticed of how far we are.

I said, strain-locus, & 'rest.' Now what is so crazy about a poem right now is how many points of balance it has, how many tilts & pushes, shoves nosings dyings speeds accelerations it can have. And holes – by which I mean non-events, "times" in which 'nothing' happens. Which I'd call rests. That is, suddenly the field of construction is a field as experience itself! What's happened, that this is possible? What are these tips but workings against strains? What is the poem but an immense contrast to any previous creation – I mean every time one works? What are these openings shut-outs amassments flip-ings etc. etc. delicacies come from?

The answer is already made. I have only put a name on it. It may be helpful. A strain-locus, for example, is only a character of any actual occasion, that through it all the strains which exist, prior present & future, in it as a 'thing,' are literally knowable as herein 'located.' A poem, then, can be, if called & seen as a strain-locus, as appropriation of the straight lines, flat loci, & time factors of anything it now is, including the tensors of sound each word it uses then make a new 'world' of (an occasion being no less than whatever algae or brown kelp in 'life' used to discover herself, and began.

I do no more than hint. The work of analysis exists. The possibility of the poem, with the quantitative let in, is all I care for. The vocabulary should set some poets free.

***

Quantity is not a category (as it was to Aristotle, and has been in Western thought since, including the minds of physicists). It is made up of immovable occasions or entities.[24]

The prejudice of the conceptual must give way at least to allow that creation is dipolar – that it is physical as well.[25] And for a terribly au fond & impressive reason (which has been much lost since Ionia): the actualities <u>have</u> to be felt, while the pure potentials (because they are mental, no matter that they are the other half, the cold pole) <u>can</u> be dismissed. This is a great distinction between an actual entity and an eternal object. A poem is made up of both.[26]

Flow, for example, is not continuous 'length,' it is leaped atomism – quanta, jumping, like nerves in fatigue – which is rightly sought & used as a habit because it has a survival value: it is a physical memory. And physical memory & causation spring from the same root: they are both physical perceptions. A poem must do equal justice to atomism, to continuity, to causation, to memory, to perception, to quantitative as well as qualitative forms, and to extension (measurable existence in field). The most important active or creative import of quantity, <u>extension</u> itself.[27]

There is a spatial element in any smallest part of a word as well as a temporal element: you measure its 'time' (as accent/pitch/speed in relationship – or, 'rest') but it matters how you cut, even cut the syllable, you have the particle of it as such, as particle, measurable quantum. They 'weigh' in time (duration); they also occupy (occur) as any thing they are felt, as they are heard.

One could trick out this side of it in a rewrite this way. Stress the advantage as against the more familiar continuous motion we inherit, of sound: the voicing or hearing of an amount of sound is not continuous, it happens step by step (or leap) each step being the hearing or voicing of an <u>amount</u> of sound no matter how small here called the quantity.

But quantity has a double aspect: its 'physical' or morphological and its genetic or 'growth' (in the fullest sense, of flow, in the universe – 'rhythm,' as rhein, as well as meter – 'wave' as well as particle.

I am purposely, in this "Part" of the discussion of <u>Projective Verse</u>, leaving the more 'physical' (physiological) out of it both as of time in the poem, and 'space' in it (the poem as object). I <u>believe</u> Part I did more with that; but in any case here the measurable (the metric) rather than sensation (more accurately physical in the particle is emphasized (feelings). The reason is a good enough one – the submerged 4/5th of the physical is 'geometrical,' technically one can put it: the physical, of time or space, presupposes quantity & not as substance (what they are) but as a measure of intrinsic, intensive & 'clear,' what lies under, available to feeling, which is belief.

There is so much to be examined on both levels. This alone is reason to do no more now than to urge attention to quantity – then some will write it, and find out the problems. For example, 'rest,' or what amounts in our art to both traction and silence ("spaces," in the poem's sounds). It actually is only another face of duration. One is continuance in place, the other in time. But they are both continuance. I supposed in the old days one would say one gives way to motion & the other to change of sound. But neither of these determinates are at all relatively in the form of the experience of present practice.

And how timbre comes forward (as against pitch?) And "attack"? The matter is rather, as pitch has got – not the words of instruments to be played: But as stand-ins of things: how to make them sound, as they do?

I have tried to state the formal properties of the quantitative.

One ought to be able to do this. But the actual experience cannot be defined or explained. It belongs to itself. What makes it worth doing, as well as formally seeing it as a possibility, is the new relationships, unrealized in our experiences and unforeseen by our imaginations, which make their appearance, & thus through the poem introduce into the universe new types of order.

***

Like the man sd, "there isn't anything in the world which is inert fact, everything is there for feeling: it promotes feeling; and it is felt. And there is nothing which belongs merely to the privacy of one individual's feeling. All origination is private, but what has been thus originated publicly pervades the world."

Quantity is both extensive and intensive. In terms of the poem, for example, because all is vector no single thing (even syllable or letter) doesn't tip on a balance reaching to the farthest out, outside the poem – way out, from the poet's, say, own sensibility, if he is poised to be that inclusive (for which read aware). Which immediately shores (extensivity does) the decisiveness of the poem's bounds. What it includes is a decisive factor of what it excludes – how it hangs delicately in the midst of any object, surveying them. The poem's <u>boundedness</u> (what declares the inside of it, its volume) has to be complete, in a sense denied to all outsideness.[28] A vague sense of externality in the poem will not do, it betrays not a high-grade organism, in the poet. The component variations in the poem have, in such a case, failed to differentiate themselves into grades of intensity.

But intensity is not only qualitative (as we have had the poet's nerves in poems, his sensitivity without any other thrust, any imbalance than his selectivity, which will do no more than arouse our admiration, to distinguish among sensations being itself a sort of triumph). Quality is a quality (power of pitch, say, to take a clear triumph). It lends itself to intensities. But the pattern of intensive quantity lends itself to the qualities, is the 'body' of them, what I have elsewhere called what lies under.

What one is talking about in quantity in verse is the power of the submerged 4/5ths – how extensivity sits in there, unobserved. But yet, to the poet, needing fully practiced – that flow (rhythm is rhein, to flow) behaves here so that the universe, as well as the individual poet, is present, and asserting its force. One could 'weigh' this whole matter but because things do flow, quantity is impetus, and thus as complete in lure as the shimmer of song.[29] The syllable (the particle – the letter) is wave and particle, at once either, each. Flow, for example, in the new metric, is not continuous 'length' (duration, or rest, continuation in time or place). It is leaped atomism, quanta jumping like nerves in fatigue – which is rightly sought and used as habit because it is a survival value: it is physical memory. Physical memory and causation spring from the same root: they are both physical perception.

A poem has so many things to which it must do equal justice if it is to establish its own bounds (be inclusive). They can be summarized (and my intent here is to say it all): atomism (that sounds, at no smallest point ain't also particles, as both said & heard); continuity (that old flow still flows, even though statement can no longer be an adequate syntax to it – wave is wave of something at all points, both the particle and, because it is a thing, its 'environment' – what, its passing through, it is different by as well as what it catches up, what adheres to it); causation (but not that moralistic one – the Coleridgian – of fact & reason; cause in physical sensation, the obverse of which – what lies under it – giving it its allowance at all, that the systematic geometries occur superficially as the face of, cause); memory (than whom there is still no muse more, the more that things, in their retention, put more demand on the poet than merely his 'own' material, shall we say); perception (of which the same extension as of memory needs to be emphasized – that the conceptual, no matter how 'mental,' and as such the dipolar to perception, still a powerful discrimination is basic, it is this, the actualities <u>have</u> to be felt, while the pure potentials <u>can</u> be dismissed. This is the great distinction between an actual entity (nothing is there except for feeling) and an eternal object (Idea). A poem is made up of both.

Add the literal quantitative, as well as qualitative forms, and the power 'extension' (measurable existence in field) and one has the inclusion. The vibratory character of the poem and itself as the 'potential' – as shoving over reality, by its coming in, as once more laying the whole thing forward (natura, said the De Broglies, does nothing but leap – natura non sed saltus) is insured.[30]*

*The extensive relations do not make determinate <u>what</u> is transmitted; but they do determine conditions to which all transmission must conform. They represent the systematic scheme which is involved in the real potentiality from which every actual occasion (of which a poem is made up) <u>arises</u>.

The weakness of poems is what they do not include. It is the narrowness of the evidence on which they rest. It is the lowgrade inspection of the poet, the failure to get out far enough to recognize the judge ('redeemer or goddess of mischief' who arises out of the nature of things.[31] Both belong at the seat of the poem – inspector and judge – if it is to have evidence, and play adequately upon the (wit)ness of the body, any of our bodies, throw us, shift us, keep us, in balance. For this is where we sense it all, in the strains there, in that locus, as the poem has been locus. How you have been shaken/taken. A poem 'rests' in its strain-locus, and we do, in it, if we are able to 'trust' same. Which

35

means that it has made itself capable of more than, involved as we are, we are. This is its light / its 'rest' is its light. And it comes from 4/5ths only the poet has got in. No matter how skillful the poet may be – in pitch, in speed (change-up), in the manipulation of the two factors accent and non-accent (old quantity) if the poem does not have a submerged if bounded quantity ('jumping' from the fish in the sea) it isn't one. The quote is at hand:

> "The reality of the rest and the enduring motion of
> physical objects (the fish in the poem's sea) depends
>   on the spatialization of the occasions (how they
> wheel) of which it is made up
>   in (and here we are back to the power of the
> differentials, especially the integral impetus, and
> what it is catching as it goes through its localisms)
>   in the historical routes of those occasions" (the
> [salinity?] of the track of the sea, the import of
> sauce on the tongue[32]

V.

There is so much to be said. Let this be it, for the moment. I would like to have said more about eliminations, and intersections (the negative of why the poet leaves out, so little practiced; as well as how, what he does get in, is tied like mortice (Whitman said); how after quantity, as intensive, is blind, and as such is what Keats was after, in his guess & oxymoron Negative Capability.[33] He was not talking of the subjective. He was talking of the subject, the poet, made object – "servant" of the poem, made negatively, by obverse, capable. Passing, Literally. His example was a roomful of children. The poet, where is he, in the poem? (etc) to free from him

---

What I have done, in the foregoing is to race into the area, for now, some applied pure thought. And it should be evident to anyone who knows him that I have completely appropriated words and means of stating them belonging to Alfred North Whitehead. It has this advantage: to have introduced into verse aesthetics, in which only Dante, so far as I am aware, has written with steady appeal, a system of thought which throughout itself makes a like appeal to common sense.

#

Etc to
Whitehead's it, (the advantage of, the present

(Endnotes)

1   Both proposition 1 and 1.1 derive from Whitehead's chapter entitled "Strains": "It is the mark of a high-grade organism to eliminate, by negative prehension, the irrelevant accidents in its environment, and <u>to elicit massive attention to every variety of systematic order</u>. For this purpose, the Category of Transmutation is the master-principle. By its operation <u>each nexus can be prehended in terms of the analogies among its own members</u>, or in terms of analogies among the members of other nexus but yet relevant to it. In this way the organism in question suppresses the mere multiplicities of things, and <u>designs its own contrasts</u>. The canons of art are merely the expression, in specialized forms, of the <u>requisites for depth of experience</u>" (*PR*, 317, Olson's underlining). In the first draft of "Projective Verse II," the reference is clearer: there, Olson writes, "the poem's job is to elicit massive attention to the variety of systematic order in creation," retaining the phrases "elicit massive attention to" and the "variety of systematic order." Also of note, in the margins of his copy of *Process and Reality*, Olson draws a line from the "to" in "to elicit massive attention to every variety of systematic order," and the line runs to the top of the page where Olson inserts "the egotism of creation is."

2   Olson's contrast between lucidity and obstructiveness appears in his annotations in *Process and Reality*. While discussing the processional forms of the universe and the modes whereby humans attempt to measure these forms, Whitehead writes, "There is a systematic framework permeating all relevant fact. By reference to this framework the variant, various, vagrant, evanescent details of the abundant world can have their mutual relations exhibited by their correlation to the common terms of a universal system. Sounds differ qualitatively among themselves, sounds differ qualitatively from colors, colors differ qualitatively from the rhythmic throbs of emotion and of pain; <u>yet all alike are periodic</u> and have their spatial relations and their wave-lengths. The discovery of the true relevance of mathematical relations disclosed in presentational immediacy was the first step in the

intellectual conquest of nature. Accurate science was then born. Apart from these relations as facts in nature, such science is meaningless, a tale told by an idiot and created by fools" (*PR*, 327, Olson's underlining). Below this, Olson annotates,

Presentational immediacy and symbolic transference
    objective form   (subjective form
                                    emotional
                                    appreciative
                                    purposive (But as the source of the
emergence of a world at once lucid, and intrinsically of immediate worth (cf. 462)

The term "obstructive" derives from Whitehead's chapter entitled "The Ideal Opposites." There, Whitehead details the obstructive nature of experiencing the passage of time: "In the temporal world, it is the empirical fact that process entails loss: the past is present under an abstraction. But there is no reason, of any ultimate metaphysical generality, why this should be the whole story. The nature of evil is that the characters of things are mutually obstructive. But the selection is elimination as the first step towards another temporal order seeking to minimize obstructive modes. Selection is at once the measure of evil, and the process of its evasion. It means discarding the element of obstructiveness in fact" (*PR*, 340, Olson's underlining). Then, toward the close the chapter, Whitehead posits the final opposites of his cosmology: "In our cosmological construction we are, therefore, left with the final opposites, joy and sorrow, good and evil, disjunction and conjunction – that is to say, the many in one – flux and permanence, greatness and triviality, freedom and necessity, God and the World. In this list, the pairs of opposites are in experience with a certain ultimate directness of intuition, except in the case of the last pair. God and the World introduce the note of interpretation" (*PR*, 341, Olson's underlining). Across the page, Olson annotates, "lucid and intrinsically of immediate worth [creation] the good in the act that it has to rename 'soul' [defined as the mutually obstructive character of things."

3   Olson discovered the term "least action" while reading Whitehead's discussion of Einstein's use of classical physics' "principle of least action." At the end of the chapter "Measurement," Whitehead summarizes, "The modern procedure, introduced by Einstein, is a generalization of the method of 'least action.' It consists in considering any continuous line between any two points in the spatio-temporal continuum and seeking to express the <u>physical properties of the field as an integral along it</u>" (*PR*, 332, Olson's underlining). After Whitehead outlines Einstein's method, he disputes the idea of measuring "the physical properties of the field as an integral" because "it is usual to term an 'infinitesimal' element of this integral by the name of the element of distance. But this name, though satisfactory as a technical phraseology, is entirely misleading" (*PR*, 332). Instead of distance, Whitehead proposes "impetus, suggestive of [the integral's] physical import" (*PR*, 332).

4   Olson here refers to Riemann's 1851 lecture: "the questions about the infinitely great are for the interpretation of nature useless questions. But this is not the case with the questions about the infinitely small. It is upon the exactness with which we follow phenomena into the infinitely small that our knowledge of their causal relations essentially depends" (*Nature*, 12).

5   The entirety of the third proposition employs terms, already cited in note #3, which derive from Whitehead's chapter titled "Measurement." The full quote from *Process and Reality* is critical for grasping Olson's use of Whitehead: "the fact is neglected that <u>there are no infinitesimals</u>, and that a comparison of finite segments is thus required. For this reason it would be better – so far as explanation is concerned – to abandon the term 'distance' for this integral, and to call it by some such name as '<u>impetus</u>,' suggestive of its physical import. It is to be noted, however, that the conclusions of this discussion involve no objection to the modern treatment of ultimate physical laws in the guise of a problem of differential geometry. <u>The integral impetus is an extensive quantity, a 'length.'</u> The differential element of impetus is the differential element of systematic length <u>weighted with the individual peculiarities of its relevant environment</u>. The whole theory of the physical field is the <u>interweaving</u>

of the individual peculiarities of actual occasions upon the background of systematic geometry. This systematic geometry expresses the most general 'substantial form' inherited throughout the vast cosmic society which constitutes the primary real potentiality conditioning concrescence (*PR*, 332-333, Olson's underlining).

6   Olson takes this emphasis on "inspection" and "judgment" from Whitehead's chapter "The Extensive Continuum," specifically where Whitehead discusses Descartes' *Meditations*. In part IV of the chapter, Whitehead writes, "Descartes also asserts that 'objects yet more simple and more universal, which are real and true' are what the 'images of things which dwell in our thoughts' are formed of. This does not seem to accord with his theory of perception, of a later date, stated in his *Principles*, Part IV, 196, 197, 198. In the later theory the emphasis is on the *judicium*, in the sense of 'inference,' and not in the sense of *inspectio* of *realitas objectiva*" (*PR*, 76, Whitehead's emphasis). At the close of Whitehead's chapter, Olson annotates, "Judicium / inspectio: Whitehead defines as immediate / induction!" Then Olson draws a line from "inspectio" and annotates a string of fragmented notes: "an inspectio of the realitas objectiva in the prehensions," "a judicium which calls into play the totality of one's experiences beyond the prehension," "cf: God as Judge, pg 478," "inspectio is instant....analysis: the speed of "it" time," and "Judgment is the principle sphere.....as we get it." Interestingly, these fragments reference the final passage of *Process and Reality*, which discusses judgment, Whitehead's cryptic "redeemer or goddess of mischief," and the dual, primordial/consequent nature of God: "Throughout the perishing occasions in the life of each temporal Creature, the inward source of distaste or refreshment, the judge arising out of the very nature of things, redeemer or goddess of mischief, is the transformation of Itself, everlasting in the Being of God. In this way, the insistent craving is justified – the insistent craving that zest for existence be refreshed by the ever-present, unfading importance of our immediate actions, which perish and yet live for evermore" (*PR*, 351). Olson underlines the entire passage.

7   Olson took the term "rest" from Whitehead's chapter entitled

"Strains": "The meaning of the term 'rest' is the relation of an occasion to its strain-locus, if there be one. An occasion with no unified strain-locus has no dominating locus with which it can have the relationship of 'rest.' An occasion 'rests' in its strain-locus" (*PR*, 319; Olson's underlining). At the bottom of this page and stretching across to the next page, Olson writes, "cf below: 468: it is not a duration (which is a rest and depends on its physical content [the rest does]; the strain-locus depends merely on its geometrical content." Then, he annotates, "a strain-locus is a creation of the possibility of and for 'rest.'" For Whitehead, a "strain" is "a feeling in which the forms exemplified in the datum concern geometrical, straight, and flat loci," his projective geometry outlined in proof form before the chapters entitled "Strains" and "Measurement" (*PR*, 310).

8   Both quotations are cited in note #5.

9   For Whitehead, "occasions," or what he also terms "actual occasions" and "actual entities," are "the final real things of which the world is made up. There is no going behind actual entities to find anything more real. They differ among themselves: God is an actual entity, and so is the most trivial puff of existence in far-off empty space. But, though there are gradations of importance, and diversities of function, yet in the principles which actuality exemplifies all are on the same level. The final facts are, all alike, actual entities; and these actual entities are drops of experience, complex and interdependent" (*PR*, 18).

10   Pertinent passages in *Process and Reality* discuss "vector feeling," and Olson follows Whitehead's use of the term in the chapter entitled "The Subjectivist Principle": "Thus the primitive experience is emotional feeling, felt in its relevance to a world beyond. The feeling is blind and the relevance is vague. Also feeling, and reference to an exterior world, pass into appetition, which is the feeling of determinate relevance to a world about to be. In the phraseology of physics, this primitive experience is 'vector feeling,' that is to say, feeling from a beyond which is determinate and pointing to a beyond which is to be determined" (*PR*, 163; Olson's underlining).

11   Olson transcribes this quotation from the opening of
Whitehead's "Strains" chapter, pg. 310 of the Griffin/Sherburne Edition.

12   Traditionally, scientists and empirical philosophers have
divided "quantity" into two metaphysical categories – extensive and
intensive – by which humans measure the universe's qualities. Extensive
quantity includes the measurement of static properties like length, while
intensive quantity includes the measurement of changeable properties
like pressure. Whitehead's chapter on "Measurement" argues that no
systematic theory of measurement is possible because "The minds of
physicists are infected by a presupposition which comes down from
Aristotle through Kant. Aristotle placed 'quantity' among his categories,
and he did not distinguish between extensive quantity and intensive
quantity. Kant made this distinction, but considered them both as
categoreal notions. It follows from Cayley's and von Staudt's work that
extensive quantity is a construct (*PR*, 332; Olson's underlining). From
"extensive quantity is a construct," Olson draws a line to the bottom of
the page and annotates "true relativism."

13   Olson refers to the epigraph to the <u>Maximus Poems</u> and
to Robert Creeley, "the figure of outward," when he discusses going
"outside the poem – way out." Butterick's *Guide* provides the relevant
lines: "the Figure of Outward means way out way out / there: the /
'World,' I'm sure, otherwise / why was the pt. then to like write to
Creeley / daily? To make the whole thing / double, to / objectify the
existence of an / Outward? […]" (*Guide*, 3).

14   Robin Blaser's essay, "The Violets," cites from Olson's copy
of *Process and Reality* and explicates the annotations relevant to this
passage. The quote from *Process and Reality*, cited by Blaser, reads, "The
inside of a region, its volume, has a complete boundedness denied to
the extensive potentiality external to it. The boundedness applies both
to the spatial and the temporal aspects of extension. Wherever there
is ambiguity as to the contrast of boundedness between inside and
outside, there is no proper region" (*PR*, 301). After citing this, Blaser
transcribes the annotation Olson attached to Whitehead's definition

of a bounded region thus: "The inside of a poem, its volume, has a complete boundedness denied to the extensive potentiality external to it. The boundedness applies both to the spatial and temporal aspects of extension. Whenever there is ambiguity as to the contrast of boundedness between inside and outside, there is no proper poem" (Qtd. in *The Fire*, 222).

15   "Intensity" is an important feeling in Whitehead's scheme, and at the outset of the chapter entitled "The Order of Nature," Whitehead identifies "four grounds of order functioning in reality." Olson's reference in his essay pertains to the second ground's "gradations of intensity":

(i)   That 'order' in the actual world is differentiated from mere 'givenness' by introduction of adaptation for the attainment of an end.

(ii)   That this end is concerned with the gradations of intensity in the satisfactions of actual entities (members of the nexus) in whose formal constitutions the nexus (i.e. antecedent members of the nexus) in question is objectified.

(iii)   That the heightening of intensity arises from order such that the multiplicity of components in the nexus can enter explicit feeling as *contrasts*, and are not dismissed into negative prehensions as *incompatibilities*.

(iv)   That 'intensity in the *formal* constitution of a subject-superject involves 'appetition' in its *objective* functioning as superject. (*PR*, 83; Whitehead's emphasis)

From the word "contrasts," Olson draws a line to the bottom of the page and writes, "contrasts as great possibilities." Then, below that he writes, "the transformation" drawing a line to the very bottom of the page where he adds "redeemer or goddess of mischief, judicium is the judge arising from the very nature of things, of final paragraph pg 497."

16   It appears as if Olson considered two other concluding lines, both of which he writes after the anecdote about Plato. The first reads,

"Whitehead is – you know the consolation of Philosophy." And the second reads: "Whitehead's it (the advantage of a philosophy in the present. It makes us Ionian."

17   Olson's reference to "extensions" derives from the title of part four of *Process and Reality*, "The Theory of Extension." Usefully, John Locke defines the term in the *Essay Concerning Human Understanding* under the heading "*space and extension*": "space considered barely in length between any two beings, without considering anything else between them, is called distance: if considered in length, breadth, and thickness, I think, it may be called *capacity*: the term extension is usually applied to it" (69; Locke's emphasis). "Extension" signifies three measurements that objectify the space between things, and Whitehead's "theory of extension" is, essentially, a theory of scientific measurement that employs geometric axioms to establish a system of measurement without using infinitesimals like a point or the number one.

18   Here Olson refers to one of his annotations in *Process and Reality*. Writing on page 221 of the Griffin and Sherburne Edition, page 312 of his copy, Olson outlines a brief thematic map of the three volumes of the *Maximus Poems*:

initial data	to	objective datum
Max 3	via	Max 1
The 'place' (as	Max 2	the poem

Environment of
Stuff observation   The subject as prior (causa sui)
                            Excluding (negative prehensions)
                            + surviving (pressing on after the poem)

19   Olson would have found the term "enduring object" in his reading of Whitehead's "four grades of actual occasions." On the opening flyleaf of his copy, Olson directs himself to Whitehead's four definitions: "First, and lowest, there are the actual occasions in so-

46

called 'empty space'; secondly, there are the actual occasions which are moments in the life-histories of enduring non-living objects, such as electrons or other primitive organisms; thirdly, there are the actual occasions which are moments in the life-histories of *enduring living objects*; fourthly, there are the actual occasions which are moments in the life histories of enduring objects with conscious knowledge" (*PR*, 177; my emphasis).

20   Early in *Process and Reality*, Whitehead writes of "strain" and "strain-locus" thus: "a certain state of geometrical strain in the body, and a certain qualitative physiological excitement in the cells of the body, [which] govern the whole process of presentational immediacy. In sense-perception the whole function of antecedent occurrences outside the body is merely to excite these strains and physiological excitements in the body" (*PR*, 126). Olson annotates this passage on the opening page of the "Strains" chapter.

21   Olson draws his emphasis on "power" from Whitehead's discussion of John Locke in *Process and Reality*: "But Locke, throughout his essay, rightly insists that the chief ingredient in the notion of 'substance' is the notion of power. The philosophy of organism holds that, in order to understand power, we must have a correct notion of how each individual actual entity contributes to the datum from which its successors arise and to which they must conform. The reason why the doctrine of power is peculiarly relevant to the enduring things, which the philosophy of Locke's day conceived as individualized substances, is that any likeness between successive occasions of a historic route procures a corresponding identity between their contributions to the datum of any subsequent actual entity; and it therefore secures a corresponding intensification in the imposition of conformity" (*PR*, 56, Olson's underlining).

22   Olson takes both of the quotations from page 310 of the Griffin/Sherburne Edition, the "Strains" chapter.

23   Here Olson twists Whitehead's passage. In the "Strains" chapter, Whitehead points out that strains between occasions cause growth, and the measurement of growth falls within the realm of mathematics: "But the growth of physical complexity is dependent on the growth of ordered relationships among strains. Fundamental equations in mathematical physics, such as Maxwell's electromagnetic equations are expressions of the ordering of strains throughout the physical universe" (*PR*, 311, Olson's underlining).

24   See note #12.

25   Olson's use of the term "dipolar" references Whitehead's speculations on God. In the "Final Interpretation," part five of *Process and Reality*, Whitehead writes, "Thus, analogously to all actual entities, the nature of God is dipolar. He has a primordial nature and a consequent nature. The consequent nature of God is conscious; and it is the realization of the actual world in the unity of his nature, and through the transformation of his wisdom. The primordial nature is conceptual, the consequent nature is the weaving of God's physical feelings upon his primordial concepts (*PR*, 345; Olson's underlining).

26   Whitehead makes this distinction early in *Process and Reality*, writing, "That an eternal object can be described only in terms of its potentiality for 'ingression' into the becoming of actual entities; and that its analysis only discloses other eternal objects. It is a pure potential. The term 'ingression' refers to the particular mode in which the potentiality of an eternal object is realized in a particular actual entity, contributing to the definiteness of that actual entity" (*PR*, 23). It should be noted that an "eternal object" is not the same as an "enduring object," discussed in Note # 19. For Whitehead, an enduring object is an actual concrete thing, whereas an eternal object is an idea or potential. Also, at the bottom of the page on which this passage appears, Olson annotates, "Consciousness not necessarily involved in how one feels or eliminates either actual entities or eternal objects."

27 · Olson links his poetics to Whitehead's cosmological perspective and defines what might be called a "cosmo-poetics." Borrowing each term from Whitehead, Olson only changes the word "cosmology" to "a poem": "cosmology must do equal justice to atomism, to continuity, to causation, to memory, to perception, to qualitative and quantitative forms of energy, and to extension" (*PR*, 239).

28   See Note #14.

29   Multiple references to Whitehead's vocabulary and his writing occur in this passage. For a definition of "impetus," see note #5.

Additionally, at the outset of the chapter entitled "Process," Whitehead cites Heraclitus: "That 'all things flow' is the first vague generalization which the unsystematized, barely analyzed, intuition of men has produced. It is the theme of some of the best Hebrew poetry in the Psalms; it appears as one of the first generalizations of Greek philosophy in the form of the saying of Heraclitus; amid the later barbarism of Anglo-Saxon thought it reappears in the story of the sparrow flitting through the banqueting hall of the Northumbrian King; and in all stages of civilization its recollection lends its pathos to poetry" (*PR*, 208).

The term "lure" references Whitehead's notion of a "lure for feeling," which he defines while discussing subjective action: "This subjective aim is not primarily intellectual; <u>it is the lure for feeling. This lure for feeling is the germ of the mind</u>" (*PR*, 85, Olson's underlining). "Subjective ways of feeling," Whitehead continues, "are not merely receptive of the data as alien facts; they clothe the dry bones of the flesh of a real being, <u>emotional, purposive, appreciative</u>" (*PR*, 85, Olson's underlining). At the bottom of the page, Olson annotates, "note how feeling (as lure) and mind as germ or expectation [...] of the subject to his own private synthesis / and whitehead sees emotion, purpose, and appreciation as secondary [...] 'subjective forms.'"

30   Unlike the earlier reference to Whitehead's list of the elements to which cosmological though must do justice, cited in note #23, here Olson includes Whitehead's final point about vibration. The full passage

reads: "cosmology must do equal justice to atomism, to continuity, to causation, to memory, to perception, to qualitative and quantitative forms of energy, and to extension. But so far there has been no reference to the ultimate vibratory characters of organisms and the 'potential' element in nature" (*PR*, 239).

31   See Note #6.

32   Olson quotes from Whitehead's "Strains" chapter: "The reality of the rest and the motion of enduring physical objects depends on the spatialization for occasions in their historic routes" (*PR*, 321). Again, for a definition of the "integral impetus," see note #5.

33   In referring to the "negative" and "eliminations" here, Olson is not just discussing Keats' concept of negative capability, but also Whitehead's notion of "negative prehension," the process whereby high-grade organisms eliminate elements of the cosmos from their attention: "It is the mark of a high-grade organism to eliminate, by negative prehension, the irrelevant accidents in its environment, and to elicit massive attention to every variety of systematic order" (*PR*, 317).

Works Cited

Blaser, Robin. *The Fire: Collected Essays of Robin Blaser.* Berkeley: University of California Press, 2006.

Butterick, George. *A Guide to the Maximus Poems.* Berkeley: University of California Press, 1981.

Locke, John. *An Essay Concerning Human Understanding.* ed. Kenneth P. Wrinkler. Cambridge: Hackett Publishing Co., 1996,

Olson, Charles. *The Maximus Poems.* ed. George F. Butterick. Berkeley: University of California Press, 1997.

---. *Collected Prose.* eds. Donald Allen and Benjamin Friedlander. Berkeley: University of California Press, 1997.

---, and Donald Allen. *Poet to Publisher: Charles Olson's Correspondence with Donald Allen.* Vancouver: Talonbooks, 2003.

Riemann, Bernhard. "On the Hypotheses which Lie at the Bases of Geometry." trans. William Kingdon Clifford. *Nature,* vol. VIII, No. 183, 1998 (14-17),

Whitehead, Alfred North. *Process and Reality.* eds. David Ray Griffin and Donald Sherburne. New York: The Free Press, 1978.

Item #00476, *Process and Reality.* Charles Olson Research Collection. Archives & Special Collections at the Thomas J. Dodd Research Center, University of Connecticut Libraries.

Box 34, Essays: "The Principle of Measure in Composition by Field: Projective Verse II." Charles Olson Research Collection. Archives & Special Collections at the Thomas J. Dodd Research Center, University of Connecticut Libraries.

Box 34, Essays: "The Poem is a Presented Duration." Charles Olson Research Collections. Archives & Special Collections at the Thomas J. Dodd Research Center, University of Connecticut Libraries.

Note on the Editor

In August of 2008, Joshua S. Hoeynck completed his Ph.D at Washington University in St. Louis, writing a dissertation titled *Poetic Cosmologies: Black Mountain Poetry and Process Philosophy*, which explores the epistolary relationships between the Black Mountain Poets and their relation to Whitehead's philosophy. While sifting through Olson's archive and investigating letters and annotations, he discovered Olson's unpublished essay "Projective Verse II," which appears here for the first time. He recently published an article on "Projective Verse II" with *West Coast Line* and is currently revising the proofs of an essay on Robert Duncan and Denise Levertov, which will appear in *Process Studies*. He also teaches freshman writing, introduction to poetry and several night classes at Washington University in St. Louis.

Note on the Author

Charles Olson (1910-1970) was a central figure in Post-World War II American poetics. Well known for extending the free-verse principles posited by Ezra Pound and William Carlos Williams, he also brought his own interests in cosmology, mythology, and community to bear on American Letters. His seminal essay, "Projective Verse" appeared in 1950 and became a key part of the principles guiding the Black Mountain Poets and the Beat Generation. Though scholars traditionally point to Olson's prose as an important contribution to literature, his magnum opus, *The Maximus Poems*, reveals his full cosmological, mythological and historical vision. There, the discerning reader will access the local fishing history of Gloucester Massachusetts, the geographical history of the planet, developments in physics and astronomy, or even Mayan myth, just a brief sampling of Olson's extensive references and interests. He died in 1970 at the age of fifty-nine, leaving a major legacy in poetry and prose that continues to fascinate, provoke and bewilder contemporary poetry.

About Chax Press

Chax Press was founded in 1984 by Charles Alexander as a creator
of handmade fine arts editions of literature, often with an inventive
and playful sense of how the book arts might interact with innovative
writing. Beginning in 1990 the press started to publish works in trade
paperback editions, such as the book you hold. We currently occupy
studio space, shared with the painter Cynthia Miller, in the Small Planet
Bakery building at the north side of downtown Tucson, Arizona. Recent
and forthcoming books by Alice Notley, Barbara Henning, Charles
Bernstein, Anne Waldman, Tenney Nathanson, Linh Dinh, Mark Weiss,
Will Alexander, and many more, may be found on our web site at *http://
chax.org*.

Chax Press projects are supported by the Tucson Pima Arts Council, by
the Arizona Commission on the Arts (with funding from the State of
Arizona and the National Endowment for the Arts), by The Southwest-
ern Foundation, and by many individual donors who keep us at work at
the edges of contemporary literature through their generosity, friendship,
and good spirits.

This book is set in Claude Garamond's eponymous typeface primarily in
10 and 11 point sizes. Composition and design in Adobe InDesign.